Why I
Follows Day

Adapted from a
Native American legend

Retold by Marlene Perez
Illustrated by Craig Smith

Long ago, the animals had a meeting to decide how long night and day should be.

2

They put Bear in charge
of the meeting.

3

Some of the animals wanted
to have the sun all the time.

Some of the animals wanted
to have the moon all the time.

The animals couldn't agree,
and they began to fight.

6

"Stop!" said Ground Squirrel.
"Let's not fight anymore.
Why don't we have night follow day?"

Ground Squirrel pointed to
Raccoon's tail. "Night can follow day
like the dark rings follow
the light rings on Raccoon's tail,"
she said.

"That's a great idea!" said Wolf.

Bear was not happy.
"No," he growled.
"It should be night
all the time."

He pushed Ground Squirrel
with his paw.
His claws made a mark
on Ground Squirrel's back.

13

But the other animals liked
Ground Squirrel's idea.

They wanted to split night and day evenly.

15

And that is why
ground squirrels have stripes,

and why night follows day.